WAR AT HOME AND AT THE FRONT

Comprising

AT THE FRONT: THOUGHTS AND PRAYERS
FOR THE FIGHTING FORCES

"A Chaplain"

1940

MOTHERS IN WARTIME

Mrs Blundell of Crosby

1942

CATHOLIC TRUTH SOCIETY
PUBLISHERS TO THE HOLY SEE

We will pray for God's mercy in the night, for his light in our dangers and difficulties next day… We will pray for our dead. We will pray for peace…

Theresa Blundell was the daughter of the theologian WG Ward, and married the head of one of England's oldest Catholic families.

CTS ONEFIFTIES

Originally published as *At the Front: thoughts and prayers for the fighting forces* by "A Chaplain", 1940; and *Mothers in Wartime*, 1942.

Published by The Incorporated Catholic Truth Society,
40-46 Harleyford Road London SE11 5AY

www.ctsbooks.org

All rights reserved.

Copyright © 2017 The Incorporated Catholic Truth Society.

ISBN 978 1 78469 547 7

AT THE FRONT

A Chaplain

AT THE FRONT

THOUGHTS AND PRAYERS FOR THE FIGHTING FORCES

BY A CHAPLAIN

FOUR POINTS

(1). **Try to realize that God is always with you.** He is with you wherever you are, and you can always pray to Him. You can always pray to Him, even if you are miles away from a church or a priest. Ask Him confidently for what you need, and He will always hear you and give you what you ask, and much more besides. He is a good Father and you are His children. And when you are in pain or in trouble, He is nearer to you than at any other time.

And so put away all fear and anxiety. Say to yourselves: "God is my helper, whom shall I fear?"

(2). Should you commit in the future a grievous offence against God, remember that **you can be reconciled to Him at any time** by a good act of contrition. It is not difficult. Tell Him that because He is so good you love Him and are sorry you have offended Him. Tell Him that you are resolved to go to Confession when you have the opportunity, and never to sin again, God Himself will help you. He is always willing to take you back. For He Himself has said: " There shall be more joy before the angels of God on one sinner doing penance than on ninety-nine just who need not penance."

(3). **Be regular in your daily prayers.** All things that are important to us must be done regularly. We have to eat regularly, and sleep regularly, and take exercise regularly in order to keep ourselves in health. And in the same way in order to keep our souls in health we must pray regularly. Every day we ought to think of God. Every day our soul needs a fresh supply of God's grace. And so make up your minds that you will say at any rate some prayer every day, even if it is only an Our Father and a Hail Mary. You can pray when you are walking about by yourself, or at your work, or before you go to sleep at night. Put yourself first in the presence of God, and say the prayers as well as you can in the circumstances. Or you can say still shorter prayers such as: "O my God, I am sorry for my sins. Jesus Son of God have mercy on me. My God, I trust in Thee alone. Father, not my will but Thine be done."

(4). Lastly, if you want to keep out of mortal sin and to serve God faithfully, **you must go to Confession and Holy Communion as often as you can.** You are not likely to be able to go once a week or once a month, as you could in peace time, and so it is all the more important that you should use the opportunity when you get it. For you will be in greater need of the Sacraments than you were in civil life. You will be living in most intimate contact with non-Catholic men. Most of your companions will probably be non-Catholics. They will not have the Catholic idea about the sinfulness of impurity. They will not care at all about the life to come or the supernatural. Mind their example does not lead you to sin. At times temptation to sins of the flesh will be thrown across your path. And you will need the support of God's grace in order that you may bear with patience and without shrinking the hardships of a soldier's life.

The Sacraments are the most sure means that we have of strengthening our soul. If a man cannot get to them through no fault of his own, then God will help him in other ways. But a man who can use them and will not, has no right to expect God to help him, any more than a sick man can expect to get well who will not do what his doctor tells him.

HOLY SCRIPTURE: GOD AND THE SINNER

Luke, c 19, v 10. The Son of Man is come to seek and to save that which was lost.

Matt., c 9, v 13. Learn what this meaneth, I will have mercy and not sacrifice: For I am not come to call the just but sinners.

Isaias, c 55, vv 6, 7. Seek ye the Lord while He may be found, call ye upon Him while He is near. Let the wicked forsake his way and the unjust man his thoughts, and let him return to the Lord and He will have mercy upon him: and to our God for He is bountiful to forgive.

Ezekiel, c 18, vv 21-23. But if the wicked do penance for his sins which he hath committed and keep all my commandments and do judgment and justice, he shall live and shall not die. I will not remember all his iniquities that he hath done: in his justice which he hath wrought he shall live. Have I any pleasure at all that the wicked should die? saith the Lord God: and not that he should return from his ways and live.

CONFESSION

I expect that some of you who read this book have not been to confession for a long time, perhaps for many years. Well, the longer the time that you have been away, the more important it is that you should go now.

Do not be afraid of going to confession because you have not been for a long time. It is **not really difficult** to make a good confession. It does not matter if you've forgotten how to begin, or can't think of what to say when you get into the box. And it isn't necessary to spend a long time trying to remember your sins. No man is expected to remember **all** the sins that he has committed. You are only bound to confess the grievous ones. And it is not difficult for a man to remember his grievous sins even though he may not remember the number of times he has committed them. And the priest will always help you, if you ask him, by asking you questions; and if you answer truthfully and as well as you can at the time, the questions that he puts to you, you will have made a good confession. Tell your sins, then, as well as you can; be ready to perform the penance the priest will give you; but above all be truly sorry for your sins and determined to give them up in future.

And consider what an **important** matter confession is for you. A soldier has to go frequently into the danger of death. Perhaps he has to remain in the danger of death for long times together. He cannot, therefore, be a good soldier if he is afraid to die. But if he has grievous sin unforgiven on his soul, then how much must he dread appearing before God. But if, on the other hand, he is in the grace of God, then there is no reason why he should fear to die. On the contrary, he knows that God will welcome him, and that death for him will be the beginning of a new and better life.

HOLY SCRIPTURE: THE MASS

I Cor. xi, 23-24. For I have received of the Lord that which also I delivered unto you, that the Lord Jesus, the same night in which He was betrayed, took bread, and giving thanks, broke, and said: "Take ye and eat: this is My Body which shall be delivered for you: this do in remembrance of Me."

I Cor. xi, 26. For as often as you shall eat this bread, and drink this chalice, you shall show the death of the Lord, until He come.

THE MASS

You cannot expect to have Mass regularly now. And so when you do get it, make a special effort to hear it well. Remember what your Faith teaches about the Mass. Nineteen hundred years ago the Son of God came down from heaven on to the earth, and lived amongst men, and died for them upon the cross. To-day, during this Mass, when the priest says the words of consecration, He will come down again, as it were, from Heaven on to the earth, to be amongst you.

Jesus will be present on this altar as Priest and Victim. Once he offered Himself on Calvary to suffer and to die; for all eternity He remains a Victim "to make intercession for us." Make a complete offering of yourselves in union with Him, saying, "Father, not my will but Thine be done."

When the priest holds up the Sacred Host at the Elevation, adore Him with your whole heart. Look up at the Sacred Host, and say, " My Lord and my God."

In the Mass we ask God for what we need in the name of His Beloved Son who is praying with us. "Amen, amen, I say to you: if you ask the Father anything in My name, He will give it you." (John xvi. 23.)

Jesus said to His Apostles: "Watch and pray, lest you

enter into temptation." That is to say, unless we watch and pray we shall be overcome by temptation.

"Simon, Simon," said Our Lord on the eve of His Passion, "behold Satan hath desired to have you, that he may sift you as wheat. But I have prayed for thee, that thy faith fail not" (Luke xxii. 31). Let us also pray that our Faith may not fail. Let us pray that we may not deny or be ashamed of our religion before men, as St Peter was led to deny Christ through fear of men. Let us pray that we may keep away from temptation to sins of the flesh, and that we may at once turn from it when it is put before us. Let us pray that we may bear patiently for God the hardships that we have to suffer.

And let us pray also for others: for our dear ones at home; for all who have lost their lives in the war; for the intentions of our Holy Father the Pope, that God may put an end to the war and give us a just and lasting peace.

HOLY SCRIPTURE: THE LOVE OF GOD AND TRIBULATION

No tribulation can separate us from the love of Christ

Rom. viii. 35, 37. Who then shall separate us from the love of Christ? shall tribulation? or distress? or famine? or nakedness? or danger? or persecution? or the sword? But in all these things we overcome because of Him that hath loved us.

PATIENCE IN SUFFERING

Hardships by themselves do not make a man better or worse. All depends on how he takes them.

Take the case of two soldiers, both of whom have to suffer the same hardships. Both have to work until they are tired out, to go and live in the trenches, to suffer cold, damp, and hunger.

One of them takes these hardships in a good spirit. He sees he has to put up with them, and so he makes as little of them as possible. He says to himself: "It is God's will." He does not cry out about them, he bears them patiently, he is even cheerful.

The other man takes them in a bad spirit. He feels bitter about them, and he gives way to this bitterness. He is angry with God for letting such things happen to him. He curses continually. He abuses his superiors, and hates and envies all those who suffer less than himself. He is always trying to do as little as he can.

The result is that the first man is made by his hardships better and stronger and holier. The second comes out of them worse than he was before. And yet both had the same hardships to go through; the second, although he tried to shirk, could get off with very little less than the first.

Let us make up our minds that we at any rate will bear our hardships in the right spirit. Let us remember that whoever bears suffering patiently in this life will receive a great reward from God in Heaven. Let us all say to ourselves:

I will take this for my sins. This shall be part of my purgatory.

By the providence of God we are now leading a hard life. We cannot make it less hard. A great opportunity is now given us of earning for ourselves a high place in heaven—much higher than we should be able to get in ordinary times—and of atoning for our sins. It would be a sad pity if we were to miss it. We **must** suffer, as things are; let us suffer well!

HOLY SCRIPTURE: SINS OF THE FLESH

Fornicators shall not possess the Kingdom of God

I Cor. vi. 9, 10. Do not err: neither fornicators, nor idolaters, nor adulterers, nor the effeminate, nor liers with mankind, nor thieves, nor covetous, nor drunkards, nor railers, nor extortioners shall possess the Kingdom of God.

I Cor. vi. 15. Know you not that your bodies are the members of Christ? Shall I then take the members of Christ and make them the members of a harlot? God forbid!

PURITY

"For know ye this and understand that no fornicator, or unclean, or covetous person (which is a serving of idols), hath inheritance in the kingdom of Christ and of God." (St Paul's epistle to the Ephesians, v. 5.)

One of the great difficulties St Paul had to fight against in dealing with the early Christians was the sin of impurity. These Christians were nearly all converts from paganism, and the sin of impurity was very common among the pagans. Indeed they hardly thought it was wrong at all. Many of the stories told about the pagan gods and goddesses are impure stories; and impure acts are even said, to have been part of some of the ceremonies of their religion.

There is no sin about which it is so easy for men to deceive their consciences as the sin of impurity. The temptations to this sin are, in the case of the majority of men, the most vehement of all temptations; moreover, they come often, and they do not go away after they have been rejected once, but keep on as it were knocking at the door of the soul. The consequence is that men left to themselves and without the help of grace are unable to overcome them. They may overcome them once or twice, but cannot do so persistently. And finding this to be the case, they give up trying and persuade themselves that in giving way to these temptations they are doing what is natural and right. All the time they have an uneasy feeling in their conscience that they are doing wrong, but they try to smother it, and this is true of great numbers of non-Catholic Englishmen of to-day. They talk and behave as though impurity were no sin at all.

So Saint Paul warns the Christians to whom he is writing that they must not deceive themselves. If they commit impurity and the other evil acts he has mentioned, they cannot at the same time be followers of Christ; they cannot obtain the kingdom of heaven.

"Let no man deceive you with vain words," trying to make you believe that what is really evil is good. "For because of these things cometh the anger of God upon the children of unbelief." God is angry with the pagans for their sins of impurity and punishes them for it although they hardly know what they are doing. How much more, therefore, will He punish you who know what you are doing. "Be ye not therefore partakers with them."

WINTER HARDSHIPS

I want to put before you a few considerations that should console you when you are suffering the hardships of winter. Many of you, perhaps, are more afraid of these than you are of being under fire from shells and bullets.

So when you are feeling cold, wet, and low-spirited, comfort yourselves with these thoughts.

First, remember that there is a reason for your enduring them. You have to do so in order to defeat the enemy, and to save your own country from the evils that he would bring upon it. And warfare in winter in this climate means living in cold and wet. It cannot be helped. These hardships may be lessened, but they cannot be avoided altogether.

So say to yourselves: I am going through this for my country, for my wife and children, for my family, for my friends, to protect them from the enemy.

A second thought. You may be feeling uncomfortable, but at any rate you are doing your duty. You are doing your duty as a soldier, obeying orders. You are doing your duty to your country, defending it against the enemy.

And inasmuch as you are doing your duty to your country, you are doing a good work for God. You are doing the will of God. And doing the will of God is what we were made for. And it is the only way to get to heaven.

And so when you feel cold and miserable, say to yourself: My conscience is good, at any rate. By being here I am doing my duty, I am serving God, I am earning Heaven for myself.

Lastly, put before yourself the example of Jesus Christ. Jesus Christ was the Son of God, and the only perfectly good man there has ever been. Yet He had to endure cold and many kinds of hardship. He was born in a stable on a winter's night. It must have been very cold there. His Foster-father and His Blessed Mother were poor people. When He was living with them, He had often felt the cold as poor people do. And afterwards, when He had left them to carry out His work, He had no home at all, not even a place to lay His head.

So too with the Saints. Many of the Saints used to go

about without enough clothes. They ate hardly any food. They slept on planks or on the bare ground.

Jesus Christ and His Saints had to suffer these things before they could enter into their glory. And we too must suffer before we can get to Heaven.

St Paul says: "No one shall receive a crown unless he has properly fought for it": that is, unless he has borne adversity bravely. But he adds, to comfort us: "The sufferings of this time are not worthy to be compared to the glory which is to come."

And so, if you are pierced right through with the cold and damp, say to yourself: I am suffering now like Jesus Christ did, when He was scourged at the pillar and crowned with thorns. Only His pains were much worse than mine. I will bear mine patiently as He bore His. And by this I shall earn my crown and come to be with Him in heaven.

PRAYER IN TIME OF HARDSHIP OR DIFFICULTY

Eternal Father, I believe that Thou art with me always. In the cold and wet Thou art with me, in the darkness as in the light. Thou knowest my heart: Thou knowest what I suffer, what I fear, what I love and desire. Thou knowest wherein I am weak and wherein I am strong. Help me, Father, to do what I cannot do without Thee.

Heavenly Father, I have often disobeyed Thee. I have

fled from pain and labour. I have loved pleasure too much. I have let my flesh many times overcome me. Father, I will not shrink from the pains, labours, dangers that are now before me. They are Thy will. I will embrace them. I am stronger than my flesh and will conquer it, with Thee and for Thee.

Jesus, Son of God, Thou lovest me. I have not kept Thy word. Thou knowest, I have been unfaithful and, left to myself, will be unfaithful again. Thou seest my heart, yet Thou lovest me still. Jesus, Thou didst suffer greatly for me and for all men. I am now going to suffer a little. I wish to suffer like Thee: not to complain: to say with Thee: "Father, Thy will be done." Jesus, my Master, I will take up my cross and follow Thee, that I may be with Thee in Thy Kingdom.

Holy Mary, Chosen and Blessed of God, who didst say: "Be it done unto me according to Thy word," pray for me that I may give myself to God, Holy Mary, whose soul was pierced with anguish to see Thy Son crucified, pray for me that I may suffer bravely. Holy Mary, Mother of Jesus and my mother, pray for me that I may come through all dangers safely and remain faithful to Thy Son.

All ye Saints of God, Martyrs, Confessors, Virgins, who have passed through many tribulations, pray for me.

HOLY SCRIPTURE: GOD'S PROVIDENCE

Matt. c 10, vv 19-21. Are not two sparrows sold for a

farthing: and not one of them shall fall on the ground without your Father? But the very hairs of your head are all numbered. Fear not therefore: better are you than many sparrows.

Matt. c 7, v 11. If you then being evil know how to give good gifts to your children, how much more will your Father who is in Heaven give good things to them that ask Him.

God is good to all His creatures

Ps. 144, vv 14-17. The Lord is faithful in all His words and holy in all His works. The Lord lifteth up all that fall and setteth up all that are cast down. The eyes of all hope in Thee, O Lord, and Thou givest them meat in due season. Thou openest Thy hand and fillest with blessing every living creature. The Lord is just in all His ways and holy in all His works.

He hears the prayers of the just

Ps. 144, vv 18-20. The Lord is nigh unto all them that call upon Him: to all that call upon Him in truth. He will do the will of them that fear Him: and He will hear their prayer and save them. The Lord keepeth all them that love Him but the wicked He will destroy.

He helps the needy and the oppressed

Ps. 145, vv 5-9. Blessed is he who hath the God of Jacob for his helper, whose hope is in the Lord his God: who hath made heaven and earth, the sea and all things that are in them. Who keepeth truth for ever: who executeth judgment for them that suffer wrong: who giveth food to the hungry. The Lord looseth them that are fettered: the Lord enlighteneth the blind. The Lord lifteth up them that are cast down: the Lord loveth the just: the Lord keepeth the strangers. He will support the fatherless and the widow: and the way of sinners He will destroy.

He knows all things and is with us everywhere

Ps. 138, vv 5-7-12. Behold, O Lord, Thou hast known all things, the last and those of old: Thou hast formed me, and hast laid Thy hand upon me. Whither shall I flee from Thy face? If I ascend into heaven Thou art there: if I descend into hell, Thou art present. If I take my wings early in the morning, and dwell in the uttermost parts of the sea: even there also Thy hand shall lead me and Thy right hand shall hold me. And I said: Perhaps darkness shall cover me, and night shall be my light in my pleasures. But darkness shall not be dark to Thee and night shall be light as the day: the darkness thereof, and the light thereof, are alike to Thee.

GOD'S PROVIDENCE

Heavenly Father, nothing can happen to us without Thy knowing it and permitting it. Thou knowest what we can do; Thou wilt help us to do what is beyond our natural strength. "I can do all things in Him who strengtheneth me" (Phil. iv. 13).

What is easy to one man is difficult to another. Each man has his own special difficulties. He must not expect others to understand them. "For every one shall bear his own burden" (Gal. vi. 6). Let him be content to bear his trials in secret. "Thy Father who seeth in secret will repay thee" (Matt. vi. 4).

THE SUFFERINGS OF JESUS

"Because Christ also suffered for us, leaving you an example that you should follow his steps" (I Peter ii. 21).

Jesus, Son of God, Thou wast often tired with walking and with Thy labours.

Thou wast hungry.

Thou didst suffer thirst.

Thou didst suffer cold.

Thou wast thought a fool.

Thou wast abused and misrepresented.

Thou wast falsely accused.

Thou wast insulted and struck.

Thou wast **made a prisoner.**

Thou wast left alone with Thy enemies, who did what they would with Thee.

Thou wast struck and bruised in many places.

Thou wast scourged with heavy rods.

Thou wast made to carry a load too heavy for Thee.

Thou wast wounded in Thy hands.
>in Thy feet.
>in Thy side.

Thou didst suffer piercing and long-continued pain.

Three hours Thou wast dying and suffering great pain.

In all this Thou didst not complain.

Thou didst obey Thy Father.

For the glory that was set before Thee Thou didst despise the pain and shame.

BEFORE ACTION

A leader must train his men as carefully as possible before the action. He must study the ground: he must exercise his powers of foresight to the utmost. But when all this has been done he cannot be sure of victory.

A man may stumble and cause a clatter and so give the alarm. The general upon whose genius and spirit the whole army depends may be killed by a stray shot. A sudden storm may flood the roads and render them impassable for troops and guns. A mist may arise and hide the enemy's positions from view. Such things as these may cause failure to the most carefully planned attack.

It remains with God to give victory to this side or to that.

HOLY SCRIPTURE: GOD AND VICTORY

The Psalmist says, speaking in the name of the Jewish people:

Ps. 43, vv 1-4. We have heard, O God, with our ears, our Fathers have declared to us: The work Thou hast wrought in their days and in the days of old. Thy hand destroyed the Gentiles, and Thou plantedest them: Thou didst afflict the people and cast them out. For they got not the possession of the land by their own sword; neither did their own arm save them; but Thy right hand and Thy arm, and the light of Thy countenance; because Thou wast pleased with them.

vv 7-8. For I will not trust in my bow: neither shall my sword save me. But Thou hast saved us from them that afflict us: and hast put them to shame that hate us.

God has not promised us victory, as He did the chosen people, but we pray that He will give it to us.

PRAYER FOR VICTORY

Almighty Father, we pray Thee, give us victory. We fight that justice may be done: that Thy will may be done. Drive from us all evil desires and thoughts that we may be worthy to find favour in Thy sight.

For if Thou art against us these will not avail us anything. But if thou art with us, even if the enemy be ten to one, we shall conquer.

Thou canst bring the strongest warrior to nought. Thou didst drown Pharaoh's army in the Red Sea. Thou didst slay Goliath with David's sling and stone. Thou didst destroy in one night the hosts of Sennacherib. Grant that we also may conquer in Thy name.

We do not trust in our own strength, in our guns or courage or strength of arm.

We offer to Thee our bodies, our lives. It is better to die now in thy grace than to live many years and die apart from Thee.

FOR OUR DEAD COMRADES
From the Ritual

Let us pray for our comrades who have been taken from us, and especially for those who have been killed suddenly, without time to prepare themselves for death.

We commend to Thee, O Lord! the souls of these Thy servants, and beseech Thee, O Jesus Christ, Redeemer of the world, that as in Thy love for them Thou becamest man, so now Thou wouldst vouchsafe to admit them into the number of the blessed. Remember, O Lord! that they are Thy creatures, not made by strange gods, but by Thee, the only true and living God; for there is no other God but Thee, and none can work Thy wonders. Let their souls find consolation in Thy sight and remember not their sins, nor any of those excesses which they have fallen into, through the violence of passion and corruption. For although they have sinned, yet they have always firmly believed in the Father, Son, and Holy Ghost; they have had a zeal for Thy honour, and faithfully adored Thee, their God, and the Creator of all things. Remember not, O Lord, we beseech Thee, the sins of their youth and their ignorances; but according to Thy great mercy, be mindful of them in Thy heavenly glory. Let the heavens be opened to them, and the angels rejoice with them, that being freed from the prison of the body, they may be admitted into the glory of Thy heavenly kingdom, through the grace and merits of Our Lord Jesus Christ, who with Thee and the Holy Ghost, liveth and reigneth One God, world without end. Amen.

"RENDER TO CÆSAR THE THINGS THAT ARE CÆSAR'S, AND TO GOD THE THINGS THAT ARE GOD'S."

By "Render to Cæsar the things that are Cæsar's," Our Lord means that we must do our duty to the Government even though it is a non-Catholic or pagan one. We must pay our taxes, perform our ordinary duties as citizens, and help to defend it.

You do not need to be told that you must give to Cæsar what is due to him. You are for the present the servants of Cæsar, that is of the King and his Government. You spend all your time working for him, and in return you receive from him your pay, your food and clothes, and other necessaries of life. And you are not likely to disobey his orders in any important matter. The consequences of disobeying orders in the army are very unpleasant; and, besides, you all get into the habit of obeying them.

But you need to be reminded of the second half of Our Lord's precept: "Render to God the things that are God's." That is to say, render to God the worship that is due to Him; keep His commandments.

The army looks after your bodies, it gives you food and clothes for them, and does all that it can to keep you in good bodily health. But it does not care at all about your souls. Provided that you keep good discipline and do not injure your health, it does not care whether you sin or not.

You yourselves have to look after this. No one else can make you do your duty to God, no one else can do it for you. Your chaplains can only remind you of it and urge you to it. Almighty God has left it in the power of each man to choose whether he will serve Him or not.

Few men deliberately refuse to serve God and choose evil instead of good. But it is easy for a man to become careless about his duty in small things and then if he does not try and stop himself he comes to neglect it in great, and finally ceases to care about it at all.

Examine yourselves to see if this has been taking place in you.

My dear brothers, you are now serving Cæsar faithfully, rendering to Cæsar the things that are Cæsar's. See that you do not neglect the still more important duty of rendering to God the things that are God's.

THE COURAGE OF CHRIST AND HIS SAINTS

In all things we suffer tribulation, but are not distressed: we are straitened, but are not destitute: we suffer persecution, but are not forsaken: we are cast down, but we perish not (II Corinthians iv. 8, 9).

One of the reasons why the Church wishes us to practise devotion to the Saints is that we may be led thereby to imitate their virtues. Let us consider, now, for a few moments, the example Our Lord and His Saints give us in regard to one virtue—the virtue of courage.

We should be very happy men if we were not afraid of anything. When a man is sad it is generally because he is afraid of something disagreeable that is going to happen to him: pain, wounds, death, disease, poverty, the anger or contempt of his fellow-men. The less a man is afraid of these things the better he is and the happier he is. Now one of the great marks by which the Saints of God are distinguished from other men is that they were not afraid of anything.

Our Blessed Lord used to exhort His Apostles and

disciples to be brave and not to fear anything. He told them that they must not be afraid of anything that men could do to them. Men could only hurt their bodies, and they must not be afraid of that. "Amen, I say to you, my friends; be not afraid of them that hurt the body, and after that have no more that they can do."

And Our Lord not only told them that they must be brave, but Himself gave them a great example of courage. He knew that if He went on with His teaching and work according to the will of His Father, His enemies would take Him prisoner and put Him to death. He knew beforehand exactly all the pains He would have to suffer, that His friends would run away and leave Him, that he would be treated by everyone as an imposter. But He did not let himself be frightened by these things; He went on with His work and teaching just the same. He could easily have escaped even at the last moment if He had wished.

"Don't you understand," He said to St Peter, "that I could ask My Father and He would give Me at once more than twelve regiments of Angels to free Me from My enemies?" But He preferred to go through it all, and to let them do to Him whatever they wished. "Father, not My will but Thine be done." And just as He was not frightened by the prospect of His sufferings, so also He bore them bravely when they actually came. When He was scourged and when His hands and feet were nailed to the cross, He did not complain; He did not utter any sound. He did not wish that others should pity Him in His sufferings, but all the time He himself was thinking of others. The Jewish women wept to see Him suffering so much when He was carrying His cross to Calvary. "Daughters of Jerusalem," He said to them, "weep not for Me, but for yourselves and for your children."

And yet if you imagine the most painful wounds and death that a soldier can meet with, they would not be so painful as what Our Lord suffered. And His enemies kept on insulting Him all the time He was suffering and dying, which is not likely to happen to any soldier.

The canonized saints of the Church from the time of the Apostles to our own day have all followed the example set us by Our Blessed Lord. They have not been afraid of bodily pain and death. Many of the martyrs endured most terrible tortures rather than deny their faith, and they include all kinds of men, sensitive and delicate men as well as the hardy—even youths and women. The saints have not feared things that most other men, usually considered brave, still fear. They have not been afraid to be poor, to live on coarse food or hardly any food at all, in mean and filthy surroundings. They have chosen these things when they need not have had them. They have not minded being called fools by other men, and generally ill-treated; and when these things were happening to them, instead of being sad as we should have been, they have kept joyful all the time.

The example of the Saints should encourage us. It

was the grace of God that made them so brave. We can be brave, too, by the help of the same grace. The saints trusted in God. Let us ask God to give us the same trust in Him, so that we may want only to do our duty faithfully, and not be anxious at all about what is going to happen to us.

MOTHERS IN WARTIME

Mrs Blundell of Crosby

FOREWORD

In the past twenty years or so giant's strides have been made in the better understanding of children by teachers, doctors, and welfare workers, and it is a great blessing for the mother to have their enlightened help in the forming of her children's lives.

But let us realize something which appears to me to be of the first importance, and it is this: In giving children to us God gave to us, their mothers, a place in their lives which nobody else can fill. And, so that we may fill that place, He gives us a special grace which I would like to call the Spirit of Motherhood. This is the grace of a mother's state of life and she has never needed it so much as in the troubled world of to-day, when her children turn to her for the comfort, confidence, and support which she alone can give.

In a world which has come to undervalue the importance of family life, children are needing their parents now as never before. Both father and mother must take their full part in their children's lives; but it is mainly of the mother's part that I must here attempt to write. I want to try and consider our children's special claims upon our Spirit of Motherhood which prayer and courageous effort can strengthen within us to meet their need.

And if we give it to our own children in our fullest measure, we shall find it is increased within our hearts so that it is able to flow through divers channels to a hungry world.

In this little pamphlet, therefore, I want also to consider how we are privileged to help our neighbours in the problems that we share with them to-day, with special application to the problems of war-time England, and with special reference to our part, as mothers, in the campaign of the Sword of the Spirit.

We walk under the banner of Our Lady, Grace of the Way. Let us go forward with a very good heart.

MOTHERS IN WAR-TIME

Mrs. Blundell, of Crosby,
National President, Union of Catholic Mothers

CHAPTER I

I, therefore, beseech you, that you walk worthy of the vocation in which you are called.—(Ephes. iv, I.)

What is our war-time vocation? In what special ways may God be calling us to restore peace to our own homes, to our own country, and to an agonized world?

I attempt to supply a part of the answer in this very small work. Please read it critically, for each of us must do her own thinking. For I suggest that we members of the Union of Catholic Mothers have each a definite personal vocation and an equally definite vocation as members of the whole. These two vocations are so closely interwoven that they are one; they cannot work independently of one another. Let us realize what is asked of us and let us, in the first instance, take inspiration from Cardinal Hinsley's exhortation in *The Sword of the Spirit*.

"We, too, have need of a return of the spirit to newness of life, if we aspire to take our due part in the renewal or resurrection of Europe. Those rules and canons of morality, which have been obscured in the prevailing darkness, should be made to shine more brightly as well on our domestic hearths as in our markets and in our public halls, of council or of entertainment."

While these words are a challenge to each of us they also bless the original aims of the Union of Catholic Mothers to uphold the Christian laws of life and the education of our children as good Catholics and loyal citizens. The needs of to-day cry for the fulfilment of those aims for our own sake and for the sake of the whole tragic world in which we live, and for which we pray.

II

Which is our most immediate field of action?

Readers of the children's classic, *Alice-Through-The-Looking-Glass*, will remember how Alice tried to explore the garden outside Looking-Glass House, and how every path she tried only took her back to the house she was trying to leave.

"Oh, it's too bad!" cried Alice. "I never saw such a house for getting in the way! Never!"

In war-time some of us may feel like "Alice-Through-The-Looking-Glass," who wanted to leave the house and explore. We may know the urge to leave our homes in search of more exciting work outside. Let us hear more about Alice. There was a path which seemed most definitely to lead away from the house, and she determined to follow it.

"And so she did: wandering up and down, and trying turn after turn, *but always coming back to the house, do what she would.** Indeed, once, when she turned a corner rather more quickly than usual, she ran against it before she could stop herself.

"'It's no use talking about it,' Alice said, looking up at the house and pretending it was arguing with her. 'I'm not going in again yet…*back into the old room—and there'd be an end of all my adventures!*'

"So, resolutely turning her back upon the house, she set out once more down the path, determined to keep straight on…. For a few minutes all went on well, and she was just saying, 'I really *shall* do it this time—' when the path gave a sudden twist and shook itself (as she described it afterwards), and the next moment she found herself actually walking in at the door."

Now, I am all for adventure, but I believe that God plans the best adventure for each of us; if we pray and if we do some honest thinking we shall know what it is.

Let us, if we will, explore fresh avenues of thought concerning our war-time vocation. I suggest that, for most of us who are mothers, each avenue will sooner or later give a sudden twist and shake itself like Alice's path—and land us back home.

---
* Italics, mine.

It is there that the Best Adventure has been waiting for us all the time.

III

In some cases it may be right and necessary that members should take up whole-time work outside their own homes. There is the married woman who has been disappointed in her wish for children and whose husband is away most of the day. When God's providence permits this state of things it is surely intended that the childless woman should find a worthy outlet for her disappointed instinct of motherhood; it should flow through other channels according to her capacities and opportunities. Such a woman is likely to be the ideal welfare-worker in the best sense of the word. And her instinct of motherhood, denied full expression in her own home, may be expressed in a most valuable manner by her co-operation in the activities of the Union of Catholic Mothers; she can, in a definite sense, participate in the united mothership of its members; the fact that she has spare time moreover makes her able to co-operate in the organization of the movement to a degree impossible for the majority of members.

Then there are widowed mothers whose children have perhaps married and left them, and other circumstances might be suggested where married women have a real call to work outside their homes, but I think that I have by now made the principle sufficiently clear. We have great individual responsibility each to think clearly about her own particular case. And even the emergency claims of war-time must be examined with the strictest honesty. The hope of the world is our Christian home-life and only the very strictest necessity should separate the home-maker from her children; if this is unavoidable for a time she should, I suggest, pray and plan for her full-time return to them at the earliest possible moment.

But to the majority of mothers God has definitely and obviously given the Home Adventure. It is her Best Adventure, and no one else can take her place in it.

We pray that the face of the earth be renewed. But if we neglect the work of renewal offered to mothers, and to mothers alone, can we honestly pray for what we ourselves are obstructing? Our children are being formed every hour and every moment to be men and women in that new world for which we pray. Are we using the full grace of our motherhood to prepare them for it, or are we not? Are we arming them with the Sword of the Spirit, or are we not? Are we leaving "that side of things" to the school teacher, or even to chance, because we haven't faced up to our vocation, or because we want to be doing something else, and have achieved the self-deception that something else is more important in war-time? If we have fallen into this particular pitfall let us pray to be got out of it as quickly as possible.

Father Bede Jarrett emphasised this when he wrote about the younger generation in the aftermath of the

First Great War, when something of great spiritual price seemed to have gone from so many of our homes, and respect for parents and obedience to them were so often lacking.

"The excuse is sometimes made," wrote Father Bede Jarrett, "that the young folk grew up in the war without a father to look after them. That alone would not have caused the trouble. The real cause was not that the fathers were not present, but that the mothers were absent. They went to work, or were touched by their excitement, and neglected their duty because, in that pitiful phrase, they wanted 'a good time'."*

In short, they chose the Wrong Adventure and missed the Best Adventure. Let us pray for them and for ourselves; it is terribly easy to choose the second-best, and for mothers the second-best is no good at all.

IV

I do not think that Father Bede Jarrett spoke too strongly of this first responsibility of motherhood, or that I have spoken too strongly of it. But let me say this:

In most cases I think that a mother's life need not be, and should not be, lived completely within the four walls of her home. At times it is necessary that it should be. While children are small, and new children are expected, the day is not long enough for its duties. Even then it is well to take an interest in outside matters, but outside

---

* *The Catholic Mother: C.T.S.*, 3d.

activities are probably quite impossible, and would not be right. But, as children grow older, as they go to school and grow up, leisure increases, and it is in their interest that we should lead wider lives, as well as in our own.

It is also in our neighbour's interest, and here I should like to make a point which I think important. In all our contacts with other human beings we shall be immeasurably helped by those quiet, busy, difficult years when we hadn't a minute to spare from our own home life; that is to say, if we have lived those difficult years as they should be lived. The mother learns a rare unselfishness from her habit of steadily putting her children before herself; she learns spiritual insight (the best psychology) from training their minds and habits in the service of God. She practises, or tries to practise, an almost infinite patience; she works hard—very hard, she endures—she learns to pray whole-heartedly for others besides herself. In short she has responded to the grace of motherhood, and it has been increased within her "in full measure and flowing over," for the helping of her neighbour in this troubled world.

To most mothers leisure comes sooner or later, in greater or less degree. Then it is, and especially in war-time, that the mother has a difficult and very individual responsibility in determining the scope of her duties outside home life; she will consider where and how her children still need her, and she will do nothing for others which would spoil her work for them. But, given time that is really her own, there is a great deal that she can and ought to do both individually and in connection with her U.C.M. Foundation.

Only—let all of us frequently apply a touchstone to this part-time work which is so absorbing and so valuable. Do we ever find that, in responding to these fresh opportunities, we are neglecting the home opportunities? Do our homes, like Alice's house, seem to be arguing with us? And do we find ourselves thinking impatiently of them? And saying with Alice, "I never saw such a house for getting in the way."

If we feel that home is getting in the way it means that we are almost certainly spending too much time on outside work, and that we are quite certainly making the new work our chief interest, that it is lessening our home interest and may in time kill it.

All this should be changed without an hour's delay. It can be set right by a generous return of the will and of our whole selves to the Best Adventure, with a new safeguard to ensure that we shall stick to it. I suggest that when we make this return we first plan out which hours of the day should be consecrated to our home vocation; then that we deliberately allot a little more time than appears necessary. That extra time may be of the utmost value. It is then that we look round and see duties that had escaped our notice. It is then that our children discover that, after all, we are not too busy to talk to them.

V

Do you by now want to cast this pamphlet into the fire and cry: "Enough! You are setting an impossible standard for mothers!"

Well, I don't set the standard. God sets it, and the image of His own Mother is blazoned on it, and humanly speaking it is quite beyond our powers to follow it.

That is why we have and need Our Lady as our patroness, to beg for us those helps without which we can do nothing at all. That is why we are given the Sacrament of Marriage, with its graces for the upbringing of our children. That is why our Pope exhorts, encourages, and prays for us and our families. That is why the Church has blessed the Union of Catholic Mothers which was started for our needs, and for the needs of the world.

VI

The Union of Catholic Mothers was instituted that we might each realize our Christian vocation in motherhood but also that by our unity the individual should be encouraged and strengthened, first and foremost by the union of prayer. When I pray for my own family, do I also pray for our many thousand members and their families? I ought to do this because they want my prayers and because I want those thousands to pray for me.

We will remember, too, *all* mothers in our prayers; they must be made for our membership but not bounded by it. We must be one with all families in charity.

We will unite in prayer that peace may come to the world and that peace may reign amongst ourselves, in the heart of each of us and in our homes.

The importance of family prayers in this regard is tremendous and to-day our needs are so great that they bring out the fullest meaning of every prayer we say. Our perils, perplexities, and separations urge us to family unity in every possible way; may we unite more strongly than ever before in family prayer by which Cardinal Hinsley has specifically asked us to take our part in the crusade of the Sword of the Spirit.

To the Union of Catholic Mothers His Eminence has written: "Make our families prayerful and you will do much to bring back God to society and society back to God."

Shall we fail to unite, then, on every possible occasion—at Mass, in our Communions, in our Rosaries, and in the prayers that every family will say nightly, those evening prayers which are of such vital importance in our crusade, and which are also so strengthening to family unity? We will each, with all the members of the family who are still at home, make them whenever we possibly can.

We will pray for God's mercy in the night, for His light in our dangers and difficulties next day. For our absent members, who are uniting with us from far away. For those fighting, wounded, or missing in our own family and in every other family. We will pray for our dead. We will pray for peace throughout the world—and then again we will beg peace for our own homes, where we are kneeling.

As we pray at night for members of our families, present and absent, we realize how much we mean to one another, and it is good for us to feel this emotion which, at evening prayer, we turn towards God. This emotion was sanctified in the Psalms; they were written thousands of years ago but they speak vividly for us now in our wishes and prayers for one another: "The Lord keepeth thee from all evil; may the Lord keep thy soul. May the Lord keep thy coming in and thy going out."—(Ps. cxx.)

CHAPTER II

Into whatsoever house you enter, first say: Peace be to this house. (Luke, x, 5.)

I

On the cover of *The Catholic Mother*, by Father Bede Jarrett, is the picture of a young mother in simple modern clothes. She is rather too thin and the baby in her arms looks rather too heavy for her. She is standing beneath a statue of Our Lady and her Divine Son, and is looking up at them. On this cover we see also the badge of the Union of Catholic Mothers.

I wonder how many war-time mothers are praying like this, and then starting out on a new and strange way, with the heavy baby and the older children, to a new home of which they know nothing until they get there. Sometimes a mother would far rather have stayed with her husband in the danger zone, but has come away for the sake of her children. Real heroism will often be needed to adapt herself to circumstances which may involve an almost unbroken succession of pinpricks.

And it is unlikely that the family which receives her will be able to appreciate her difficulties, nor can her own children, by reason of their youth. She may also need an unusual degree of tact and patience with the children, to help them to settle down. But I do believe that we can adapt ourselves to new and difficult surroundings if we try to do so as a part of our vocation as members of the Union of Catholic Mothers, with much prayer to Our Lady, Grace of the Way.

For the mother who prays for "grace of the way" will accept her war-time trials heroically in union with all our members who are all suffering unaccustomed trials just now. Instead of a dreary endurance of daily difficulties, she will go forward cheerfully and will practise strong virtues, especially the virtue of charity. The world of to-day is apt to forget that true charity is love of God and our neighbour, and is mutual; a give-and-take in which all concerned are equally privileged, in which all concerned may thank God for the giving and the taking.

"Deal thy bread to the hungry."* The great prophet

---

* Isaias, lviii. 7.

who spoke these words did not concern himself only with loaves of bread, as is shown in the words that follow: "When thou shalt pour out thy soul to the hungry, and shalt satisfy the afflicted soul, then shall thy light rise up in darkness...."*

In almost every house that we may enter in war-time there is hunger of heart whether we at first discover it or not. It may be caused by bereavement, by loss of companionship, by anxiety, by a yearning for security. If a mother knows this hunger herself she is the better able to help her hostess, but she will not recognize the troubles of another if she is absorbed in her own. Only if she desires to "deal her bread to the hungry" will she discover who those hungry people are whom she may satisfy: "then shall thy light rise up in darkness, and thy darkness shall be as the noonday. And the Lord...will fill thy soul with brightness."†

There is also the great hunger (all the more dangerous if it is not realized by those concerned) of the family that has grown up without Faith, or the family of the careless Catholic. An evacuee member received by such a family may not indeed be able to persuade her hostess to start a new life; sometimes, even, it might not be wise to try. But help in such a case does not always depend on the "direct attack." Those who receive us into their homes will judge us daily by our kindness, patience, and adaptability; above all by the cheerful good temper

---
* Isaias, lviii' 10.
† Isaias, lviii, 10, 11.

which is a part of charity. By our faithfulness to Mass and the Sacraments, daily prayer and family prayer. By our conduct towards and with our children. And above all, by our trust in God's Providence. We shall have done much if we leave behind us when we go a mother whose life has been helped, steadied, and brightened by a member of the Union of Catholic Mothers; who will ponder on the why and wherefore, and in time realize the spiritual wounds of her own life, which realization is the first step to the ultimate healing.

In entering another home in war-time our prayer upon the threshold shall be, *Peace be to this house,* and we shall pray that our every word and action may help to bring that peace, in which we shall share, to the healing of our own hearts.

II

*"Bring the needy and the harbourless into thy house."**

Harbouring the stranger is at once a blessing and a problem. This charity towards "nobody we know" is promised a wonderful reward when we come to die, for Our Lord will say then: "I was a stranger and you took me in."† And if we have forgotten the whole thing, and answer: "Lord, when did we see thee a stranger?" He has told us His reply: "As long as you did it to one of these my least brethren, you did it to me."‡

---

* Isaias. lviii, 7
† Matt. xxv, 35.
‡ Matt. xxv, 40.

Yet it may have needed a heroic effort to sacrifice the privacy of home life by welcoming the stranger. And our visitor may be used to different ways, she may not be "our sort." But if there are drawbacks, they will not disturb our kindness of word or thought if we are beginning to realize the meaning of true charity, and of our reward that will be so infinitely greater than anything that we can give.

We shall pray for a real and steady unselfishness in our hospitality, and in time actual self-forgetfulness will set in, which will help us tremendously and will broaden our whole outlook; and may we one day make the wonderful thanksgiving expressed in Psalm twenty-seven: "The Lord became my protector, and He brought me forth into a large place."

And if we harbour the harbourless, accepting each difficulty as a means of grace from God, we shall soon realize in a very happy way how God has come to us with the stranger.

CHAPTER III

One body and one spirit, as you are called in one hope of your calling.—(St Paul, Ephes., iv.)

I

Our need for unity in prayer and sympathy and work is greater than ever before. We must give our best as individuals and pull together as a whole. And our unity will enlarge our sympathies and give us new vitality. I am a better mother if I realize that I am "not the only one"; if I understand that others are sharing in the joys and trials of the great Home Adventure; that I am praying for them, and they for me. Actually our unity extends into other countries through that world-wide organization, *Les Mères Chrétiennes,* so that we must remember the Christian families in France and in other countries and unite with them in prayer for one another and for every family in the world.

And in England let us also unite in our plans for active war-work; this unity enlarges our opportunities so that each may discover her own talents in our united effort. I am struck by the initiative and perseverance of many of our members who have worked and sympathised and prayed together undaunted by the dangers and anxieties in which we live; may we all do likewise.

If a Foundation can hold together at all it should try to continue with its Communion Day, monthly Benediction, and weekly or monthly meetings, and when possible with its work and prayer for our Forces and for all in need. And the same applies to all officers and organizers. Let us do all that we possibly can and then we can pray with confidence that God may make good all that we cannot do.

But let us be ever watchful to strengthen our corporate unity and to enlarge our membership. We can often seize most valuable opportunities just now. Some of us can even help to begin Foundations in parishes to which we have evacuated; many others can join in the activities of one which already exists in our new neighbourhood.

And may every member in a reception area join in heartfelt welcome of the evacuee mother. It is a privilege to visit her, to cheer her loneliness, to offer help if needed, and friendship always; to do all that we can if a baby is expected: all this is a splendid opportunity to give consolation and support to one who is feeling lost and lonely, and has troubles which no official organization, however excellent, can remove, but which we, as Christian mothers, can unite to heal.

II

And always, at all times and in all places, let us remember *that spiritual unity is possible even where the full corporate unity is denied*. Even if a member is completely cut off from any Foundation she must never forget this. So much can be done to remain in touch. Mass and Communion can be offered in unity with the Parish Foundation from which she is separated, which offering, of course, also unites her with the whole Union of Catholic Mothers. Work for her neighbours can be offered in the same unity. When at night she prays with her children she is praying in close union with all of us, her fellow-members. She can join, too, with all of us in offering her daily trials as sacrifice for the peace for which we pray. Soon she will feel that separation from fellow-members does not mean loneliness of spirit. Far from it. For she will strengthen her spiritual union in such a way that it will bring her nearer in spirit to them than ever before; she can indeed take heart in the united prayer and sacrifice which enriches herself and her separated fellow-members too.

The lonely mother has special need of the consolation of spiritual unity with her fellow-members, especially if she be out of spirits, out of health, over-tired, or anxious, as, after her experience of danger and difficulty, she well may be. But she never need, and she never will, forget to strengthen herself and our whole Union of Catholic Mothers by her prayers. Even if she is ill, and tried almost to breaking-point, she can say to herself the wonderful words of a modern mystical poet:

> "Where my feet refuse to take me, there will I kneel down. And where my hands fail me, there will I fold them."*

CHAPTER IV

Jesus, Mary, Joseph, I give you my heart and my soul.
—Indulgenced Prayer.

The Divine Child could have been saved from Herod by a miracle. But God chose that the Holy Family should act much the same as our families must act to-day.

I am almost startled by our closeness to the Holy

---

* *Hymns to the Church*, by Gertrude von Le Fort (Sheed & Ward)

Family in these days of peril; startled in the sense that one is shocked out of the usual habits of thought by a tremendous grace.

"Arise, and take the Child,"* was the angel's message to Saint Joseph, and we, too, are called to arise and take our children to safety, whether to air-raid shelter or to another home. Like the Holy Family, too, our journeying is dangerous, so we must be sure to travel in Their company; this should make us very calm; nothing can happen to us that They do not permit. And when we shall come back again, when those are defeated who sought to destroy us, may we never for one moment have parted company with Jesus, Mary, and Joseph.

Without them we mothers cannot even begin to attain the Spirit of Motherhood. And our trust in Them will be the measure of our children's confidence in God.

We must face the fact that, in war-time conditions, this confidence may be weakened or re-enforced by us. If the child has had startling experiences, or has been upset by the tragedies of others, he may well be puzzled as to why God allows all these horrible things. He may not ask this question of his mother, for he will probably be ashamed to have thought of it at all. He may stifle the puzzled feeling, but it will stay below the surface of his mind and he won't, in consequence, keep his full trust in God, which he is going to need his whole life through.

If we have the Spirit of Motherhood we shall almost

---
* Matt., ii, 13.

certainly discover if our children are puzzled in this manner, and encourage them to talk. A small child can understand a great deal if his mother explains it to him and if he feels he can explain his own thoughts to her.

Let him understand that God Himself has made nothing that is evil, He can only make good things. But a great many people have refused His good things because they are proud and greedy and want power. This has brought war and suffering.

That good people are trying to be extra good in wartime to make up to God for the bad people and the pain they cause Him. Also that they are being extra good in hopes that, if He is pleased with them, He will have mercy on the world.

That God is longing to give His good things again, but that He wants us to ask for them. He wants the poor, bad people to have them too, but first they must be sorry for their badness.

The child will pray that they may be sorry and may turn to God.

The child will be reminded that the Holy Family had to run away from danger, just as we have; that They understand our troubles and will guide us and comfort us if we keep near Them. But if we are not good, if we won't keep near Them, then we shan't hear Their voices because they are too far away.

This is for the children, and it is for us too. If we

"can't think what to do," let us first examine ourselves as to how near we are to the Holy Family. We must be as close as ever we can get, or how can we hear Their voice in guidance and in consolation? If we keep near we shall hear it in our souls and make our difficult decisions rightly. Of that I am quite certain.

CHAPTER V

May the God of Israel join you together and may He be with you...and now, O Lord, make them bless Thee more fully.—From the Catholic Marriage Service.

I

Children need the Spirit of Fatherhood too. The united essence of fatherhood and motherhood must mingle in their lives. I do not think that enough is thought or said about this, and I can say but little in this very small work.

It is impossible to exaggerate the importance of this united parenthood.

The child accepts by instinct the family pattern as planned by God, and he takes for granted that his parents are united in their love for him and for one another. This sound instinct suffers a severe shock if the parents quarrel. If they "fall out" together they fall out of their right place in the family pattern and the child knows this without realizing that he knows it. His "united" protectors are divided amongst themselves; he cannot agree with both.

He cannot respect either when he hears their voices raised in anger towards one another. His peace is shattered by this, his sense of security is displaced by uncertainty, confusion, and fear.

He doesn't, of course, understand his own agitation. He only knows that daddy and mummy are quarrelling and that everything seems wrong. He is right; the family pattern is as wrong as it can be.

But God can make all things new. He can renew the pattern for us even if we have spoilt it. provided that we pray our hardest for this renewal and that we try our hardest to return to His pattern in every moment of our family life. It is true that, humanly speaking, if we have so transgressed we cannot completely undo the harm which our children's emotions have suffered, but we can and must pray with special earnestness in this regard since there is no limit to God's mercy.

Another matter is the small, passing quarrel between parents, which may be termed the "squabble." This matters far less, of course, and yet it can matter very much, especially to a highly strung child; also it tends to make quite normal children anxious and nervy. Home peace is ruffled by it and the child's instinct is again disturbed; he assumes harmony between his parents so that irritability surprises and worries him, nor can he fully respect a father or mother who are not fully respecting one another. The same applies to incivility between parents and to any form of "belittling" chaff, even if not really ill-tempered. This "belittling" chaff belittles the parents in their children's eyes; to command respect gentleness and self-control are necessary in small matters as well as in greater ones.

Some of us may not feel quite happy about this state of things in our own homes. We shall be very happy when we have put right whatever is wrong. We shall know the peace of constant cheerfulness and the fun of the joke that has no sting in it. The children will instinctively respond to the right atmosphere; they will be well-mannered among themselves and at ease with us.

We cannot, however, shut our eyes to the painful circumstances in which some lives must be lived. In certain cases the child's ideas of fatherhood may be so desecrated by the father himself that the home pattern cannot be rightly fulfilled in spite of the mother's noblest efforts. In these circumstances she will do what she can and she will pray unceasingly about the things which she cannot do. If she herself works and prays hard for her family she can be very hopeful that God our Father will Himself make good in the children's lives all that their earthly father has denied them. That she should turn to Him for this is of the greatest importance.

"May the God of Israel join you together." In what I am now about to write I want to assume that father and mother have realized this grace of the Marriage Service in their lives, in spite of occasional imperfections;

that they have united in the good things given to their children, spiritual as well as material.

In war-time we have a new problem. Fathers and mothers are separated. The mother is left alone in the home-field while the children continue to develop—faster than usual, probably, since an early knowledge of sorrow and anxiety often leads to this.

Is the Spirit of Fatherhood to have no part in the forming of their lives because daddy is away? This must not happen. It will hurt the children more than we can easily realize. By throwing out God's plan for the family, we throw out their whole sense of security and their whole adjustment to life.

Actually, a mother who is at one with her husband will, even unconsciously, keep an element of his fatherhood in the home when he is away. And may she consciously strive to keep it there in every way she can. In his absence he must yet be a vital part of home life; he must be in the atmosphere. At evening prayer the children must realize that he is with them in spirit, however distant in place, saying the same prayers and thinking of them as they are thinking of him. His wishes for them, however small, must be respected. If we change his rules and arrangements for the children without good reason we are separating them from him, and weakening his essential place in their lives.

He must not come back to find that war conditions have come between us and him. We will talk of him with our children, of what he is doing, of what he would have liked us to do in this or that matter. We will write to him often and see that the children write, too. We may dislike writing letters, but we can overcome that feeling if we know how much depends on it. How can we expect to keep him close to us if we neglect the most obvious way of keeping in touch? Children will soon respond and look forward to writing to daddy; will save up bits of news for him about treats and school successes, about what they themselves are doing to help the soldiers, and so on. He is lonely without his family; they must understand that. They must take their own part in the family pattern.

There is an old saying that absence makes the heart grow fonder. This is deeply true during the first weeks of absence, but there is a danger for some of us, as time goes on, which might in certain cases lead to tragedy. Separation will sometimes make people console themselves with interests near to hand. The father may come back to find his family absorbed in new work and new recreations; everything seems new to the poor father since he went away; he has scarcely heard of these new things and he has no part in them.

If we fail in giving him his rightful place at home, whether he is absent or present, then our motherhood will fail too; it can't be isolated from the fatherhood with which God joined it.

But what if the father never comes back? How does this affect the Spirit of Fatherhood in our home?

Fatherhood is then enshrined for us. Daddy can help

the children more than ever from heaven, because he is so near to God. He can talk to God about them and ask for all the things he did his best to give them here. Each time we pray for him and talk of him, and think of him with God our Father, the Spirit of Fatherhood is strengthened in the children's lives.

CHAPTER VI

In much experience of tribulation they have had abundance of joy.—St Paul to the Corinthians, viii, 2.

In this war there has already been much tribulation for mothers; some have lost husbands, some children, some both husband and children.

All their lives Catholic mothers have sung the *Stabat Mater* to Our Lady of Sorrows, in which they begged that they might stand beneath the Cross with her. Now they are there. They have gone further in her company than they had thought to go.

So that now, if they unite their will with hers they can share with her in God's redemption of the world.

And in the measure that they share in His Crucifixion they will surely share in His Resurrection. Even here and now this partaking of His Resurrection begins in their souls, and we wonder at the peace of these mothers who "weep as though they wept not."*

---

* Wisdom, iii, 6

But what of their motherhood if their children are gone? I think the answer is that they who stand so near to Our Lady are sharing in her Motherhood to the world. Sharing in it by their daily work and prayer for others. But above all sharing in it because they are themselves a part of God's Sacrifice for the redemption of the world.

"As gold in the furnace he hath proved them, and as a victim of a holocaust he hath received them…they that trust in him shall understand the truth…."*

---

* St Paul, I Corinth., vii, 30.

BACKGROUND

An army chaplain offers plain advice to soldiers, with particular emphasis on the usual temptations of military life: grousing at authority or physical discomfort; fear; sexual misdemeanours. Prayers and short Scripture passages are also included. This is a practical book, with no illusions about the nature of army life.

Mrs Blundell's booklet began as a talk given in 1942 to the Union of Catholic Mothers. The normal difficulties of motherhood were amplified by the particular circumstances of wartime: rationing, the systematic evacuation of children from cities under threat of German bombing; separation from husbands and fathers. Mothers should practise the peacetime virtues (patience, discernment and encouragement, prayer) but also incorporate them into the great mission of prayer called by Cardinal Hinsley "The Sword of the Spirit". She stresses the need to be united, in prayer even if not in person, with other Catholic women at home and abroad, and with husbands and fathers in peril of their lives.

CTS ONEFIFTIES

1. FR DAMIEN & WHERE ALL ROADS LEAD · *Robert Louis Stevenson & G K Chesterton*
2. THE UNENDING CONFLICT · *Hilaire Belloc*
3. CHRIST UPON THE WATERS · *John Henry Newman*
4. DEATH & RESURRECTION · *Leonard Cheshire VC & Bede Jarrett OP*
5. THE DAY THE BOMB FELL · *Johannes Siemes SJ & Bruce Kent*
6. MIRACLES · *Ronald Knox*
7. A CITY SET ON A HILL · *Robert Hugh Benson*
8. FINDING THE WAY BACK · *Francis Ripley*
9. THE GUNPOWDER PLOT · *Herbert Thurston SJ*
10. NUNS – WHAT ARE THEY FOR? · *Maria Boulding OSB, Bruno Webb OSB & Jean Cardinal Daniélou SJ*
11. ISLAM, BRITAIN & THE GOSPEL · *John Coonan, William Burridge & John Wijngaards*
12. STORIES OF THE GREAT WAR · *Eileen Boland*
13. LIFE WITHIN US · *Caryll Houselander, Delia Smith & Herbert Fincham*
14. INSIDE COMMUNISM · *Douglas Hyde*
15. COURTSHIP: SOME PRACTICAL ADVICE · *Anon, Hubert McEvoy SJ, Tony Kirwin & Malcolm Brennan*
16. RESURRECTION · *Vincent McNabb OP & B C Butler OSB*
17. TWO CONVERSION STORIES · *James Britten & Ronald Knox*
18. MEDIEVAL CHRISTIANITY · *Christopher Dawson*
19. A LIBRARY OF TALES – VOL 1 · *Lady Herbert of Lea*
20. A LIBRARY OF TALES – VOL 2 · *Eveline Cole & E Kielty*
21. WAR AT HOME AND AT THE FRONT · *"A Chaplain" & Mrs Blundell of Crosby*
22. THE CHURCH & THE MODERN AGE · *Christopher Hollis*
23. THE PRAYER OF ST THÉRÈSE OF LISIEUX · *Vernon Johnson*
24. THE PROBLEM OF EVIL · *Martin D'Arcy SJ*
25. WHO IS ST JOSEPH? · *Herbert Cardinal Vaughan*